Original title:
Saltwater and Sand

Copyright © 2025 Creative Arts Management OÜ
All rights reserved.

Author: Riley Donovan
ISBN HARDBACK: 978-1-80581-535-8
ISBN PAPERBACK: 978-1-80581-062-9
ISBN EBOOK: 978-1-80581-535-8

Shoreline Dreams

I built a castle, all out of cheese,
But the tide came in, it fell with ease.
The seagulls laughed, a comical sight,
As my cheese fortress vanished from light.

With buckets and shovels, we dig and we play,
Pretending to fish, but it's just a bouquet.
A crab grabbed my toe, thinking it a snack,
Didn't see that coming—now I'm under attack!

Shine of the Setting Sun

The beach ball bounces high with glee,
Seagulls steal fries, oh can't you see?
Kids run and tumble in the sun's warm glow,
While adults sip drinks, talking slow and low.

A crab in a speedo draws quite the crowd,
He's dancing and prancing, feeling so proud.
Flip-flops are flying, shoes left behind,
As waves crash and splash, we're all intertwined.

Sandcastles rise like dreams made of luck,
But watch for the wave, or the sand's just muck!
Shells decorate towels, treasures unbound,
While sunscreen is slathered, a sticky surround.

As evening descends, it's a real treat,
With hot dog fire-roasting, what can't be beat?
The sun waves goodbye with a twinkle and cheer,
Tomorrow we'll come back, same time next year!

Beneath the Bitter Breeze

The seagulls squawk, they jest and tease,
While crabs do kick up quite a breeze.
We built a castle, oh so grand,
But watch it crumble, just like sand!

Flip-flops fly with every wave,
A contest of who's the toughest brave.
We laugh as our snacks take a dive,
And wonder how we'll ever survive!

Ephemeral Shores

A jellyfish did tango past,
With moves that made us laugh out fast.
We chased a wave, oh, what delight,
But it kept running, like a fright!

Seashells giggle on the ground,
As we trip over, hearts unbound.
The tide pulls in, our toys will flee,
We yell, "Don't leave us with the sea!"

The Kiss of the Sea

The water whistles, a cheeky kiss,
It splashes me when I thought of bliss.
I wave hello, and wave goodbye,
As my summer hat begins to fly!

A dolphin winks, with such a grin,
While I try to catch a wave—my fin!
But in the end, I lose it all,
And land face-first, a comical fall!

Tidepool Serenade

In tidepools filled with creatures bright,
The sea stars wink in pure delight.
We tell them stories, loud and clear,
They bubble back, it's music, dear!

A hermit crab with quite a show,
Dances around, oh what a pro!
We sit and cheer, our laughter blends,
With nature's tunes, as joy transcends.

Layers of Ocean

A jellyfish floats in a lazy breeze,
With its tentacles waving like spaghetti tease.
A crab does the cha-cha with grace and flair,
While seagulls laugh loudly without a care.

The dolphins are plotting a water balloon,
While fish have a party, dancing to a tune.
They giggle and splash, causing quite the scene,
In a world of mischief where all is seen.

A Symphony of Shells

Clams hold auditions for a beachside band,
Their rhythm is quirky, it's hard to understand.
Oysters drop beats with pearls that shine bright,
While starfish show off their moves in the light.

A conch shouts a solo, loud as can be,
But seagulls critique with a squawky decree.
The performance is wild, a show quite absurd,
As the waves roll in, beckoning the herd.

Dance of the Currents

Waves take the lead in a splashy ballet,
Doing the moonwalk, they surf and they sway.
With barnacles cheering from rocks on the side,
And seaweed waving, it's a joyous ride.

The tide pulls a prank, trying to steal shoes,
While sea turtles giggle, unleashing the blues.
The ocean's a stage, where everyone plays,
In this seaside circus, laughter displays.

Whispers of the Dunes

A squirrel is sunning, a scene quite absurd,
While sand keeps on tickling, that's how it stirred.
The lizards engage in a game of charades,
As the wind joins the fun, shifting the shades.

Sandcastles lean in, sharing gossipy tales,
Of mermaids and pirates who once set their sails.
The whispers abound, in the soft evening glow,
In a sandy escapade that steals the show.

Beneath the Surface

In a place where the fish wear hats,
Sometimes they gather for chats.
A crab in a suit starts to dance,
While a shrimp takes a chance on romance.

An octopus plays the guitar,
With jellyfish singing from afar.
The clams all snicker and dunks,
While a whale throws in some funky prunks.

Lullabies of the Breaking Wave

The gulls are cawing a silly tune,
As seaweed wiggles beneath the moon.
A starfish dreams of being a star,
While a clam shouts, "Look, here comes a car!"

Seashells gossip under the sun,
About crabs who never seem to run.
A fish wearing glasses reads a book,
In hopes that the sharks will take a look.

Footprints in the Dust

The footprints lead to nowhere fast,
As seagulls dive and aim to blast.
A sandcastle loses its crown,
When waves giggle and knock it down.

A flip-flop races with the breeze,
While kids sport bucket hats with ease.
The beach ball's in a tug-of-war,
Between two kids who want to score.

Secrets of the Shallows

In the depths where the clam does hide,
There's laughter that cannot abide.
A turtle tells tales of lost flip-flops,
While a dolphin pulls off some belly flops.

The sea cucumbers whisper so low,
About how they envy the crab's show.
For beneath the waves, where the fun deploys,
The ocean is filled with quirky joys.

Nature's Textured Canvas

The beach is a canvas, oh so wide,
With footprints and shells that slither and glide.
Seagulls call out, quite the loud choir,
While kids build castles, fueled by desire.

A crab wears a hat made of jellyfish bloom,
While seaweed dancers take over the room.
Waves bring the laughter, ticklish and bright,
As sunscreen battles with sand in the fight.

Lullabies of the Lagoon

In the calm of the bay, creatures nap tight,
While fish play hide and seek, what a sight!
A clam sings a tune, off-key but bold,
As frogs croak their verses, legends retold.

Mosquitoes buzz by, they're the gatecrashers,
Making the party—a series of clashes.
Turtles poke heads, curious and slow,
As the sun sets, giving the world a warm glow.

Seaside Fantasia

Oh, the ocean's a stage, what a grand show,
With barnacles glued, that's how they glow.
Dolphins in costumes, splashing with glee,
   As jellyfish wiggle a strange melody.

The sand whispers secrets to those who will hear,
Of flip-flops forgotten, and burgers unclear.
Crabs with their pincers pretend to be kings,
As breezes laugh lightly, and the sea sings.

Driftwood Tales

Once a piece of wood, drifted afar,
Now it's a bench and a pirate's old car.
Seagulls sit plotting their next great heist,
Stealing chips from the beachgoers, oh what a feast!

With each rise of tide, new stories arise,
Of starfish detectives and crustacean spies.
They share goofy whispers, secrets so grand,
In the saga of life by the shimmering strand.

Forgotten Footprints

Lost in the grains, what a mess,
A crab scuttles by, I must confess.
My shoes left behind, in a playful way,
Now they're part of the beach, come what may.

A seagull swoops down with a squawk,
Pecking at flip-flops like it's a joke.
I chase it away, but it starts to dance,
Stealing my snacks, oh what a chance!

Footprints lead nowhere, a silly quest,
Following my dog, who likes the best.
The waves laugh hard, as I trip and fall,
A watercolor mess on the sandy ball.

Dance of the Dunes

The dunes are alive in a wiggle and sway,
I'm convinced they dance when I'm not in play.
With a shimmy and shake, they tease the sun,
As I tumble and laugh, just trying to run.

My beach ball rolls off, like it's got a plan,
It takes a vacation, away from my hand.
I chase it with joy, what a curvy ride,
While the dunes giggle softly at my wild glide.

Sandy snacks and giggles fill the air,
Bringing unwelcome crustaceans, I swear!
But a dance-off erupts, mishaps and cheer,
The dunes and I are the stars right here!

Breaths of the Breeze

The breezes whisper secrets, oh so light,
Blowing hats away as I hold on tight.
A gust lifts a kite, giving it wings,
While I'm left waving, it's just silly things.

The wind tickles noses, a swift little tease,
Sending sand in my eyes, just to please.
I squint at a crab, who finds it quite grand,
As I make silly faces at our fine land.

With every strong gust, there's laughter afoot,
As I dodge all the shells that make for a hoot!
A breeze takes the day, as I tumble in glee,
Nature's joke in the air, just laughing with me!

Currents Carrying Dreams

The waves whisper dreams in a bubbly tone,
As floaties drift by, claiming us as their own.
A dolphin leaps high, doing a flip,
I try to join in but just take a dip!

Surfboards and laughter fill the sunny day,
I try to ride one, but hey, not today!
The ocean's a tease, with its ebb and flow,
Just when I stand, it says, "Down you go!"

Currents keep dragging my snacks far away,
I chase down my chips like a child in play.
But each little splash reminds me to cheer,
In this funny tableau, I've nothing to fear!

Salted Breezes

The seagulls squawk, they steal my fries,
With beaks so bold, they claim the prize.
I laugh and wave, they dive and swoop,
    As I sit here, a salty stoop.

The beach ball rolls, it drags my feet,
A toddler giggles, what a sweet treat.
With sunscreen thick, I'm quite the sight,
    Like a pizza paste, all shine and light.

Hidden Treasures of the Coast

I found a shell, but it's just a rock,
My treasure hunting skills need to talk.
A crab scuttles by, in a hurry to flee,
While I ponder life, as he creeps past me.

Buried beneath, I spy some shoes,
Where did they come from? Guess I'll snooze.
An old flip-flop, full of holes,
Is that a gem? My mind extols.

Waves of Reflection

The waves crash hard, they play their game,
I dodge and weave, but look quite lame.
A splash here, a squish there, I laugh so loud,
My friends all point, I'm quite the crowd.

A sunburned nose, I hide with flair,
Like Rudolph, but with added care.
I strike a pose, oh so proud,
As laughter echoes, it draws a crowd.

Cliffs Beneath the Sun

The cliffs they stand, so tall and fierce,
I take a step, my bravery pierce.
A tumble, a roll, now who can tell,
If I'm a hero, or just a shell?

My buddy yells, 'Don't be a fool!'
I'm concocting plans of a cooling pool.
But here I am, with salt and grit,
The show must go on, I'll never quit!

Coloring the Shore

Crabs in tuxedos skitter about,
Trying to dance, but they just pout.
Seagulls squawk with a flair so grand,
Wishing they could play in the band.

Feet in the water, a race with a wave,
Splashes and giggles, how bold and brave!
Flip-flops flying, oh what a sight,
The sea's a playground, pure delight!

Sand castles crumble with each tick-tock,
Mermaids snicker, they'll block your clock.
Buckets and shovels, a wild parade,
Making a mess but they've got it made!

An octopus waves from under a rock,
In his weird tux, he loves to mock.
With laughter and joy, the day unfolds,
Creating memories, precious as gold.

The Poetry of the Ocean

The waves recite verses, oh so deep,
While crabs compose, they hardly sleep.
Seashells whisper secrets, bold and bright,
Each one a tale of a playful night.

A dolphin juggles with flair and style,
Splashing around, making us smile.
A clam rolls its eyes, feeling quite grand,
While the barnacles chant in a band.

Footprints run wild, then wash away,
Like a joke told and lost in play.
Sand dollars giggle, quite shy anytime,
As we frolic along, to nature's rhyme.

A wave tossed a fish with a comical flop,
It landed right next to a seaside shop.
And laughter erupts as we roll in the tide,
Where fun never settles, only tries to hide.

Embracing the Sea Breeze

The wind sings songs that tickle the nose,
Spinning my hair in ridiculous flows.
Shells tumble past like runaway toys,
As kids splash about, making all kinds of noise.

Kites soar above with flapping attire,
Dancing on currents like they're on fire.
A burly guy struggles, too proud to call,
While a seagull swoops down, making him fall.

The breeze plays tricks with my ice cream cone,
Flavors of chaos, I scream, "Oh no!"
Fingers get sticky, the sun shines bright,
As I chase errant scoops in a wild plight.

But with each gust, laughter fills the air,
As friends toss Frisbees without a care.
We shout out loud, 'tis folly, indeed,
With whimsy and joy as our hearts take the lead.

Chromatic Tide

Crayons of color spill on the shore,
Painting a landscape they'll want to explore.
The turquoise swirls with a bubblegum hue,
A genius creation, who knew?

Bright yellow fish sporting funky shades,
Having a party beneath the cascades.
While starfish giggle, all splayed out wide,
In a sunlit world, living with pride.

Beach balls zoom like comets in flight,
Chasing a breeze, oh, what a sight!
Flip-flops land where laughter is found,
In a vibrant kingdom, joy knows no bound.

As the sun dips low, all colors collide,
Creating a canvas, igniting our stride.
So let's paint the night with a spark and a grin,
In this magical realm, where fun begins.

Dunes of Time

The sun burns bright, a lively sight,
In flip-flops lost, what a silly fight!
I chased a seagull, he stole my fries,
Now I'm the one with the hungry cries.

The beach ball bounces, it hits my head,
My friends are laughing, I want my bed!
With sunscreen streaks like a modern art,
These sandy pranks steal my beachy heart.

Blue Horizons

A cloud of laughter floats overhead,
I trip on a shell, face met with spread.
The waves giggle softly, they tease my toes,
They're in on the joke, as everyone knows.

My tan lines form a pattern quite bold,
A checkerboard drama, stories untold.
With every splash, my dignity sinks,
But who needs class when the ocean winks?

Secrets Beneath the Tide

Digging for treasures, I find a shoe,
Whose foot was in this? I haven't a clue.
The fish are all laughing, they know my plight,
I'm just a beach bum, trying to get it right.

With seaweed tangled like a shoddy scarf,
My friends erupt in a fit of laugh.
I pose like a model, they snap away,
A mermaid's curse in the light of day.

Footprints in the Foam

I made my mark, right next to a crab,
He scuttled away, thought I was mad!
The foam's a prankster, it tickles my feet,
While I'm chasing laughter, what a silly feat!

With buckets and shovels, a castle I made,
But waves sneak in, just to invade.
Now I'm just left with some shells in my hand,
A sandy comedian, the punchline unplanned.

Echoes of the Shore

Waves crash with a hearty laugh,
Crabs dance like they've had too much gaff.
Seagulls squawk a silly tune,
As kids build castles in the afternoon.

Footprints lead to nowhere fast,
Someone lost their sunscreen at last.
Flip-flops flying, a beach ball's fate,
Oh, what fun, this sandy state!

The sun's a prankster, blazing bright,
While sunscreen squirted, what a sight!
Beach umbrellas flap and sway,
As wind joins in the beach day play.

Ice cream drips down hands and smiles,
While sand gets stuck for a few miles.
Shrieking laughter fills the air,
A day of joy beyond compare!

Serenity Beneath the Surface

Dolphins giggle, making waves,
While sea turtles drift and misbehave.
Underwater plants dance to the beat,
While fish share gossip, oh so sweet!

An octopus juggles with flair,
Shells serve as seats for a fishy affair.
Crustaceans hold a dance-off mad,
With the best moves that you've ever had!

The sea floor is a treasure trove,
Of shiny things that the gulls once drove.
Bubble-blowers in a sea of fun,
Painting smiles till the day is done!

Secrets of the Seabed

Sand dollars giggle in quiet disguise,
While starfish tell tales of ocean lies.
The buried secrets, so well kept,
In the waves' whispers, dreams are swept.

A clam clamors, "Don't peek, I'm shy!"
As a crab in a tuxedo walks by.
Goldfish share their glittery tricks,
In a world where laughter always clicks!

Lost sunglasses wander through the scene,
While mermaids chuckle, keeping it clean.
With bubbles popping, joy's not far,
Like seaweed dancing under the star!

Shimmering Shoreline

The tide rolls in with a funny face,
As surfboards tumble in a brisk race.
Seashells hum a tuneful refrain,
While dolphins play tag in the surf and rain.

Kites fly high, tangling with glee,
As children squeal, "Hey, look at me!"
Sandwiches vanish; was that a ghost?
As laughter ensues, they're what we toast!

Tanned legs squeak with every stride,
The beach is a carnival, come for the ride.
Ice-cold drinks spill, just add ice,
When life's this funny, you've got to think twice!

Lines in the Sand

I drew a line with my big toe,
Then watched the tide say hello.
It giggled and pulled me in,
While I tried to wipe off my grin.

The crabs stomped by in a parade,
In military formation, they played.
I tried to join, but tripped on a shell,
Now I'm a joke they all tell.

A seagull landed, stole my fries,
I yelled, 'Oi, that's not very wise!'
He winked and flew with a cheery squawk,
While I plotted my next food heist walk.

The sun set low, painted the scene,
With purple and gold, oh so serene.
As I waved goodbye to the day's fun game,
I thought, "Next time, I'll bring a name!"

Journey to the Distant Shore

On a boat made of dreams and some string,
I set out to find the next wild thing.
With a map that was drawn by my three-year-old,
I knew this adventure would never get old.

Fish in their hats waved as I passed,
I wondered how long they could last.
Caught in a net of seaweed and charm,
I thought, "This is definitely a harm!"

I spoke to a dolphin that swam too fast,
He laughed at my stories, said, "What a blast!"
With a splash and a flip, he was off in a whirl,
Leaving me here with my wonderful pearl.

The shore came near, with surprises galore,
I found a treasure, though it was just more gore.
Yet as the journey closed its goofy door,
I knew I'd be back for another score!

Aquatic Canvas

The sea is a painter with colors so bright,
Splashing fishermen, what a delight!
With each stroke, they cast nets like pro,
But often left behind their catch, oh no!

Seashells giggle as they sunbathe in rows,
While crabs throw parties in their fine, little clothes.
I joined their dance, but oh what a blunder,
I tripped on some barnacles, fell asunder!

A seagull performed, a real fine show,
Stealing my snack while I sat down low.
With crumbs on my lap, I laughed in defeat,
Next time I'll bring snacks that're hard to beat!

As the tide washed away my silly regrets,
I painted my story without any bets.
Each wave a new joke in this goofy land,
Where laughter and splashes go hand in hand!

The Splendor of the Coastline

Oh the beach is a circus, come one, come all,
With sunburned tourists ready to sprawl.
The sand tickles toes and makes them all dance,
While seagulls plot snacks with a mischievous glance.

With beach balls flying in a colorful race,
A toddler's headwear, a fishy embrace.
I tried to impress with my fabulous flip,
But landed face-first, took a dive and a dip!

The volleyball net draped in seaweed shame,
Caught in a tangle, I changed my game.
I joined the sandcastle builder brigade,
But ended up sculpting a very sad spade.

As daylight faded, the laughter grew loud,
With echoes of joy that would make any crowd.
So here's to the splendor that brings us all near,
With sandy mishaps and buckets of cheer!

Flickering Candlelight on the Waves

A candle's flicker on the shore,
Pretending it's a disco floor.
Seagulls dance with wobbly flair,
While crabs hold speed dating in pairs.

With burgers flying in the breeze,
A hungry dog begs with such ease.
A beach ball lands on someone's head,
And all those sunscreen shirts turn red!

Flip-flops squeak a silly song,
As kids shout out, "Where do we belong?"
The tide rolls in with a splashy cheer,
While a seagull steals your chips, oh dear!

So come, enjoy this wavy show,
Where laughter bursts and worries go.
With starlit skies and ocean's cheer,
You'll have a grand time, that's quite clear!

The Calm After the Storm

When clouds go home and winds relax,
The beach reveals its hidden tracks.
A sandwich lost, a soda spilled,
A hermit crab's ambitions killed.

A sunburned guy in polka dots,
Trying to charm a bunch of knots.
A dolphin peeked, then made a joke,
While jellyfish observed from smoke.

The sun now shines, but what a mess,
With sunscreen slathered, way too excess.
The lifeguard's chasing a rogue kite,
While seagulls laugh, what a sight!

As laughter dances on warm, soft air,
Forget the chaos, drop your care.
Just follow joy where it may lead,
With goofy fun your heart will feed!

Seashell Chronicles

In pockets deep, our treasures hide,
With stories from the ocean wide.
A shell that champions leafy greens,
While crabs retell their silly scenes.

"Once I surfed on a fishy wave,"
Claims one with pride, all brave and grave.
Another shells out tales from the deep,
Of midnight feasts when no one's asleep.

A starfish smiles, with gleeful cheer,
As beachcombers stumble, shed a tear.
"Did you see what that wave just stole?
My lunch, my hat, my favorite shoal?"

But laughter rules, as joy explodes,
Our cartwheeling hearts rebel from codes.
These stories crafted by seashell kin,
Join us in love and mischief win!

Drift Among the Dunes

Come wander where the sand is soft,
In dunes where laughter's always aloft.
A tumble here, a slip or slide,
Where giggles echo as we collide.

A kite takes off, but then it dips,
Right into some unsuspecting lips.
While sandcastles melt in hot desire,
Someone's lost their key, oh, what a fire!

"Not a problem!" we joyfully shout,
A crab runs by, it gives us a pout.
We race to chase this crafty fellow,
With squeals of joy, our hearts aglow.

So dance and prance on this golden shore,
Where mishaps are love, and love is galore.
In these silly moments, our spirits soar,
With laughter and fun, we long for more!

Sea Glass Wishes

Wishing on the bits of green,
The treasures found, a glowing sheen.
My dreams are washed with every wave,
Who knew I'd be so sea-glass brave?

I turned a bottle upside down,
Out popped a crab with a little frown.
He whispered secrets from the tide,
Of mermaids who forget to hide!

I thought I'd find a message neat,
Instead, I met a crabby treat.
With every wish, a giggle here,
I might just need a new career!

So here I am with bits of glass,
Wishing for a giant fish to pass.
But what if all my dreams come true?
A world of crabs, oh what a zoo!

Caught Between Tides

I'm stuck between the ebb and flow,
My feet all wet, my pants aglow.
The sun is high, the laughter's loud,
But here I am—oh lucky shroud!

I tried to run, jumped like a frog,
Slipped on a tide pool, oh what a slog!
A seagull laughed and stole my fries,
Why do they have to be so wise?

The waves keep teasing, coming near,
Like playful puppies, full of cheer.
I toss my troubles in the sea,
But they just come back, taunting me!

Caught in a game I didn't choose,
The seagull's caw, my only muse.
But hey, at least the view is great,
Life is a mess, but I'll celebrate!

Rising Sun, Falling Stars

The day begins with golden rays,
And night insists on silly ways.
A sun that rises, but what a tease,
It shines on them—the sleeping breeze!

I chased a star with ice cream cone,
It giggled, said, "You're all alone!"
With sprinkles on my sandy toes,
I thought of things, like where it goes.

Nightfall brings a blanket tight,
I hope the stars won't start a fight.
They flicker like they're playing tag,
Come on, bright ones—don't be a drag!

I'll weave a tale of sun and stars,
A dance of waters and shoes with scars.
Maybe tomorrow, they'll align,
And we can have a cosmic dine!

The Embrace of the Horizon

Oh horizon, with your smoky dress,
You wrap the sea in a grand caress.
But what a game—you're never still,
One moment near, the next a thrill!

I wave hello, you tell me, 'Chill,'
With all that distance, what a thrill!
I thought I'd visit, sit and chat,
But all I found was a sunburnt hat.

You're like that friend who always bails,
Too far to catch, you tell tall tales.
But here I stand, my toes in foam,
You're still so pretty, I'll call you home!

So here's to you, ever so wide,
With every wave, my trusty guide.
In every glance, a laugh enshrined,
Oh, horizon, always on my mind!

Sunset's Caress

The sun dips low, a golden fry,
Seagulls squawk as they float by.
A crab in the sand, oh what a dance,
He scuttles away, not missing his chance.

Flip-flops squeak, a comedic tune,
Umbrellas tip over with a cartoon swoon.
Children build castles, a sandy delight,
Till a wave crashes in, their screams take flight.

Ice cream cones drip, a colorful mess,
Moms chase down kids in a sandy dress.
A dog runs by, his tail a flag,
While a Frisbee sails, oh, what a snag!

As day turns to dusk, we laugh and cheer,
For the funniest moments are always here.
With jellyfish jokes and sunscreen fights,
We wave goodbye to those golden lights.

Whispers from the Depths

In water's embrace, the fish give a wink,
They gossip 'bout beachgoers, we can't help but think.
A mermaid with a shell phone, so cool and so sly,
She texts her fish friends, while we wave goodbye.

A lobster rolls laughter, while shrimp play the bass,
Who knew the ocean had such good taste?
Seaweed wigs bob as the tide gives a push,
While dolphins chuckle, in their speedy rush.

Pirates in flip-flops, searching for gold,
Trading sea tales that never get old.
While octopuses juggle, quite the odd sight,
We can't help but giggle, what a night!

All creatures unite for the grand ocean ball,
With bubbles and laughter, they all have a ball.
The secrets they share, like a splash of good fun,
Make us laugh harder, as the day is done.

Ocean's Whisper

The sea tells tales with a splash and a sigh,
As crabs hold a meeting underneath the sky.
A starfish sings loudly, off-key yet bold,
While hermit crabs gossip, sharing their mold.

Beach towels flutter like flags in the breeze,
As sunscreen's applied, with hilarious squeeze.
A flip-flop flops off, takes an adventurous leap,
While seagulls engage in a food-stealing sweep.

Sandcastles crumble, and laughter erupts,
While a brave little kid dons a bucket for luck.
Shells used for trumpets, a band on the shore,
Oh, the ocean's a stage, we're begging for more.

With each comical wave, the humor unfolds,
As beachgoers gather, sharing dreams and their gold.
We laugh with the tide, in this whimsical land,
Where the shore meets the sky, and life's just so grand.

Tides of Memory

The tide rolls in with a giggly wave,
A beach ball's lost, oh, how it misbehaves!
With toddlers in buckets, a wild little crew,
Chasing down waves, just me and you.

A pair of sunglasses, half-buried in sight,
Belong to a sunbather who's lost in delight.
While beach chairs tumble, like they're in a race,
The sun sets behind, with a golden embrace.

Seashells are treasures, some smooth, some quite shy,
A snail playing tag, it's a chase on the fly.
Sand everywhere; we're part of the mess,
As we hop in the waves, what a sandy dress!

With laughter and shouts, we're stamped in the sand,
Unraveling stories, hand in hand.
As night starts to fall, and the moon starts to peek,
We'll dance by the shore, sharing laughs till we peak.

Under the Vast Sky

Seagulls squawk like they own the place,
While I run from a wave in a comical chase.
My flip-flops fly, oh what a sight,
Who knew a beach day could end in a fright?

Sand lodged in my burger, oh what a feast,
Crumbs on my towel, I'm a picnic beast.
With sunscreen gone rogue, I'm a glowing red,
Next to my friend who's part crab, part bed.

The cooler tips over, it's a fizzy dream,
Cans of cola rolling, they dance and they scream.
We laugh till we cry, under sun's bright glare,
The day is a blast, without any care!

Serenade of the Shoreline

A crab in my shoe, oh what a surprise,
Wiggling around, trying to rise.
I dance like a fool, while he steals my snack,
In this comedy show, I'm under attack!

Wet dog shakes near, I'm drenched head to toe,
Why do I pick the beach for a show?
My towel's a sail, as the breeze takes its chance,
I'm flapping about like I'm stuck in a trance.

The sunburned folks rise, look like candied flames,
Just trying to hide from these silly games.
With laughter and splashes echoing wide,
This beach day adventure's a joyful ride!

The Rhythm of the Ocean

The waves crash down with a thunderous cheer,
While my ice cream melts, I'm filled with sheer fear.
Seagulls are plotting, their eyes on my cone,
They're circling like pirates, I feel so alone!

A sunburnt pirate, that's my new role,
With shades on my head, and sand in my shoal.
My friend takes a dip and yells out a tune,
While I'm fishing for snacks like a fool by the moon.

The tide rolls in, like it's late for a dance,
Dragging my chair, oh what a mischance!
But laughter surrounds like the sun's warm embrace,
In this wacky wonderland, life's a wild race!

Where the Land Meets the Sea

Where water meets land, I trip and I splat,
My hat flies away, took a dive like a cat.
With laughter erupting, I roll in the foam,
This beach is our stage, it feels just like home.

A conch in my hand, I pretend it's a phone,
Calling all seashells to gather 'round home.
But they're busy with secrets, whispers of the tide,
While I'm out here giggling, in oceans wide.

My buddies are building a castle so grand,
But it's really just rubble, end up as quicksand.
With each wave that crashes, our laughter does soar,
In the mess of this beach, who could ask for more?

Tides of Time

The ocean's waves dance, oh what a sight,
They tickle my toes, give a splash and a bite.
Seagulls fly overhead, squawking with glee,
While I try to outrun them, tumbling to see.

The beach chair I sat on just flew like a kite,
Chased by a breeze on a day oh so bright.
I laugh at my hat, now lost in the blue,
A gift for the fish, they know what to do.

Whispering Waves

A shell in my hand tells secrets galore,
It whispers sweet tales from the ocean's floor.
I lean down to listen, it yells just for fun,
"The crabs are out partying, come join us, just run!"

Buckets in tow, we make castles with flair,
Only to find that our dog ate a chair.
He digs up my snacks and buries his bone,
While I ponder if this beach life is really my own.

Embrace of the Ocean

The swell gives a hug, then a quick little shove,
It frolics like puppies, with nary a shove.
I dance with the foam, slip and fall on my rear,
The jellyfish laugh, they've got no sense of fear.

My towel tries to vanish, like a stealthy thief,
It flaps in the wind like a kite on a reef.
I chase it in circles, what a hilarious sight,
Who knew that a beach day could turn into flight?

Grain and Tide

The grains underfoot tickle like tiny wee bugs,
As I gather warm treasures, wrapped snug like big hugs.
I spot a bright starfish, it winks with delight,
Says, "All your sunblock can't stop my spotlight!"

A frisbee goes flying, it sails to the shore,
But lands on a toddler, who starts to explore.
We giggle and chuckle at this sandy surprise,
In this sandy arena, we're all in for laughs!

Emotions of a Sun-Kissed Afternoon

Seagulls squawk like they own the beach,
Chasing crumbs with a slightly loud screech.
Sunburnt noses and flip-flops askew,
While ice cream drips in a sad little stew.

Kids build castles that quickly collapse,
Towers of dreams made with giggles and claps.
A sudden wave steals their hard work away,
They laugh as they puddle in salty spray.

Sunny skies boast of a humorous game,
Where sunbathers lose their SPF fame.
And frisbees soar like comets in flight,
While someone's stuck in a towel, what a sight!

As the day ends, with shoes stuck in muck,
We leave with tales of our beachside luck.
With sand in our hair and smiley grins wide,
Life's a funny mess, come take a ride!

The Language of the Ocean

The waves whisper secrets, a cryptic laugh,
They pull us closer, then drift us out fast.
They say, 'Keep your shoes, we prefer bare feet!'
While shells giggle softly, saying they're sweet.

Crabs think they're dancers on a sandy stage,
Shuffling sideways in a graceful rage.
Each wave that crashes is a joke well-timed,
As we all chase water with laughter entwined.

Surfboards tumble, it's comedy gold,
As surfers fall in, acting brave, yet bold.
The ocean laughs loud, it's the king of jest,
With every wipeout, it gives us its best.

And at the day's end, as the sun says goodbye,
We leave with a tan and an upside-down pie.
For nothing beats humor wrapped in a sunny hue,
As waves carry whispers, just meant for me and you.

Rock Pools and Daydreams

Rock pools glisten like a painter's delight,
With tiny homes of shrimp, what a sight!
The barnacles chuckle, stuck to their stone,
While fish tell tall tales of their daring roam.

In each little puddle, a world full of cheer,
Where mermaids swim by, or they just disappear.
Kids peer in close, with noses all pressed,
Surprised by the sea life in each lovely nest.

The seaweed waves like a gooey green cloak,
As whispers of sea gnomes trigger a joke.
An unexpected hop, a splash, then a scream,
Here at the shore, you're inside a dream!

And as the tide leaves, we gather our fun,
With buckets of laughter, we say we've just won.
The day ends with giggles and grains in our shoes,
In the kingdom of rocks, there's always good news!

Timeless Alchemy of the Shore

Where land meets the sea and silliness breeds,
Joke-telling waves paint laughter like weeds.
A seagull swoops in, all confidence and flair,
Stealing a chip like it just doesn't care.

Footprints heeled in sand, like old-timey clues,
Leading us onward to mismatched shoes.
The sun gives a wink, it's a mischievous star,
While beach balls bounce like they've come from afar.

Old folks share tales of the fish that they caught,
While kids tease each other, their laughter's not fought.
The shore is a stage, with life as a play,
Where silliness reigns in a glorious way.

As the sun dips low, painting skies with delight,
We leave with our memories all sparkly and bright.
A timeless alchemy, a blend of sheer fun,
Where sandcastles and smiles will always be won!

Echoes of the Deep

A fish with a hat, what a sight!
Swimming past crabs, giving them fright.
The jellyfish dance, swing to the beat,
While starfish joke, claiming their seat.

Seagulls squawk in a comical way,
As they steal our fries, brightening the day.
With sunburned noses and ice cream cones,
We laugh like seals, our silly tones.

The waves tease us, retreating so sly,
As we try to run, oh my, oh my!
But every splash brings giggles anew,
Who needs a towel? We'll dry in the blue!

So let's wade in, splash like a fool,
Making memories, did you bring a stool?
As the tide pulls back, we embrace the fun,
In this perfect playground, we're never done!

Twilight by the Water

The sun bows down, painting the sky,
While crabs wear sunglasses, oh my, oh my!
The beach ball rolls; it hits a poor chap,
Who yells with glee, 'That's a perfect slap!'

As twilight whispers, the music starts,
Driftwood, pine cones, our creative arts.
A seagull dives for some chips on the sand,
We laugh at the sight, we just can't stand!

The sandwiches dance like they're in a trance,
While ants join the party, ready to prance.
The waves chuckle softly, a gentle tease,
As we build our castles, let's hope they don't freeze!

With laughter and silliness, we share the eve,
Telling tall tales, who could believe?
In this twilight glow, let's grip the cheer,
Tomorrow we'll return, there's nothing to fear!

The Color of Seashells

In shades of pink and orange galore,
Seashells sing songs, oh, what a roar!
We gather them up, what a funny view,
One looks like a shoe, and two like a stew!

The tide rolls in, with a giggle or two,
As we trip on our buckets, it's true, it's so true!
A mermaid lands, looking all absurd,
'Keep it down, folks! You've disturbed my herd!'

Beach towels fly like kites in the breeze,
While seagulls squawk, aiming right for our peas.
Sandcastles tumble with a final roar,
'Looks like our kingdom is now on the floor!'

We wear shells as hats, like a band of clowns,
And dance by the shoreline, in flip-flop gowns.
With laughter and joy, we celebrate fate,
Finding humor in seashells, life is just great!

Roaming the Beach

Let's roam the shore, where the wild waves call,
Dodging these puddles with our beach ball.
A crab in a tuxedo thinks it's a show,
He's strutting around like he's in a flow!

We spot a lone flip-flop, that's lost its pair,
It's waving hello like it just doesn't care.
Seagulls debate if they're wearing a coat,
As we snack on chips, we watch them gloat.

Surfers tumble with a splash and a yelp,
Learning their moves with a ghostly help.
Sand in our hair brings a stylish flare,
While pinching our noses, we jump in the air.

So here's to adventures, both silly and grand,
From quirky sea creatures to castles of sand.
With laughter aplenty, the beach is our stage,
Every moment a story, we flip to the page!

Whispered Truths of the Coast

Seagulls squawking all around,
Stealing chips without a sound.
Towels tangled, weirdly posed,
The sunburned dancers all exposed.

Shells are treasures, or so they say,
But I swear that one fled away!
Beach ball battles, oh what a mess,
Who knew splashes could cause such stress!

Flops and trips in flip-flops galore,
Trying to surf but fell on the shore.
Sand in my sandwich, salty surprise,
Why's the ocean full of sticky fries?

Chasing crabs that dart and dash,
Napping sunburned, oh what a crash!
Yet in the laughter, we find our thrill,
Coastal antics, a comedy fill.

Castaway Dreams

On an island with no Wi-Fi,
I think I heard my brain say bye.
Coconuts talk, or so they claim,
Is it the sun or me going lame?

I build a boat from driftwood found,
But now I'm just stuck on the ground.
Every wave hums a silly tune,
I'd dance with a shark, if I could croon!

Palm trees swaying, join the fun,
They're my crew, but they're all puns!
A crab stole my sandwich with a grin,
I guess I'm destined not to win.

Tiki torches flicker at dusk,
In my head, I'm a pirate—so brash!
Yet in this game of stranded bliss,
I'd trade it all for a pizza kiss.

Marshmallow Skies

The clouds are fluffy, like sweet treats,
Are they made of cream cheese and beets?
I threw a wish on a candy cloud,
Now the seagulls yell, oh so loud!

Balloons slip past like silly dreams,
Jellyfish bounce in sunlit beams.
Giggling waves tickle my toes,
I'm on the hunt for marshmallow foes!

Kites flutter high, like jokes in the air,
Why are fish always in despair?
Because they can't take a joke, you see,
Under the sun, we laugh with glee.

The sandcastles wobble, their moats won't hold,
But it's the best game, or so I'm told.
Under this sky, silly dreams fly,
With giggles and grins, we laugh till we cry.

Seafoam Serenade

Pickles on the beach, who thought of that?
A snack surprise, oh, imagine that!
While surfboards dance with grace and flair,
I try to join, but just land—beware!

Jellyfish waltz to a breezy tune,
While I trip on both feet, what a swoon!
Seashells singing, a concert of glee,
But I can't hear over my clumsy spree!

A crab in a tux poses for fame,
Snap that photo—it's surely a game!
Sand in my hair, a glorious mess,
Nature's in charge, I must confess.

Tidal waves dance like they know a joke,
I wave back, then trip with a choke.
In this watery circus, life's just grand,
With giggles and splashes, hand in hand.

Sheltered in Salt

In a beach hut that's quite small,
I thought I'd host a grand ball.
But seagulls flew in with a squawk,
And danced on tables, what a shock!

I served up snacks of sandy chips,
But all they did was steal and flip!
My guests, instead of having fun,
Just yelled at birds and on the run.

The tide rolled in, we had a splash,
I tripped and fell, not with panache!
Now my hair's a salty mop,
I guess this party just won't stop!

So here we laugh with seagull friends,
A festive night that never ends.
With salty chips under the moon,
Next time I'll just hire a spoon!

The Language of Shells

Oh the shells, they sing to me,
In a concert, wild and free.
One says 'hello,' another 'bye,'
I swear, they'll start to cry!

An oyster whispered secrets deep,
While a conch just had to leap.
'I'm a trumpet!' the clam did boast,
As I laughed and grabbed my toast.

The scallop joined in with a flip,
While I took a chip from my drip.
Who knew shellfish could be so funny?
Next thing you know, they'll ask for money!

So I leave with shells tucked away,
After all the words they say.
An undersea gossiping spree,
Come join our chat, it's quite a plea!

A Symphony of Surf

Waves crash in a rhythmic beat,
Like a marching band with sandy feet.
I tried to join with a wild dance,
But ended up getting quite a chance!

My flip-flops flew, they took a dive,
As I laughed, thinking, 'I'm alive!'
A crab waved back with a tiny claw,
I guess he didn't mind my law.

The seaweed came with a lilting tune,
Swaying gently, under the moon.
But when I tried to take the floor,
It tangled me, and I fell for sure!

So here we dance, my crustacean crew,
With jellyfish floaters, oh what to do?
Next time I'll just stick to the shore,
And hope my flips don't make me roar!

Dreams on the Estuary

In the wetland where ducks do strut,
I dreamed a lot, but fell in a rut.
I dressed as a fish, all scales and glee,
Hoping the ducks would swim with me!

But instead, they quacked and took flight,
Leaving me in a fishy plight.
I splashed around like a silly thing,
While onlookers laughed at this fishy fling.

A generous turtle blinked and said,
'Don't you know? Just go back to bed!'
But I insisted on being a pro,
Flying past all that marshy woe!

So if you see me in a blend,
With feathers and fins, just be a friend.
For dreaming's grand in the marshy light,
But it seems I'm not quite fishy bright!

Mythical Shores

Where mermaids sing with glee,
And seagulls steal your fries.
A crab steals my shoe,
While I'm busy chasing the tides.

A dolphin does a flip,
And smacks me on the head.
A whale gives me a wink,
As I trip on seaweed's bed.

With treasure maps galore,
And pirates singing loud.
I think I found a chest,
It's just a clam-shaped shroud.

Finally, I relax,
In this whimsical land.
But watch that sneaky gull,
He's plotting with the sand!

Nature's Mosaic

Painted shells like jewels,
Counting toes in the foam.
A sunburnt lobster asks,
"If squids can dance, where's home?"

Flip-flops start to vanish,
Did a fish take my pair?
I chase them down the beach,
While seagulls laugh and stare.

Kites soar like balloons,
While my hair becomes a nest.
A crab decides to join me,
Guess I've found a new guest.

Sand castles proudly stand,
Though the tide thinks it's fun,
To wash my dreams away,
So I just build and run!

Adrift in the Wet Breeze

Waves crash and everyone squeals,
As I tumble like a fool.
My sunscreen is far too thick,
I'm practically a seal!

A floatie drifts on by,
With a flamingo in tow.
I hop right on with flair,
But then it starts to go slow.

Seashells whisper secrets,
Of treasures lost at sea,
I only found some seaweed,
And a flip-flop, lucky me!

Laughter in the distance,
Something funny's going down.
A dog's wearing sunglasses,
And he's really owning the crown!